A

REFRESHING

CHUCKLE

II

31 Daily Devotionals To Kick

Start Your Day

By

Dr. CHUCK GLENN

And

B.L. GLENN

Dr. Chuck Glenn
mwy4chuck.com
contacts@mwy4chuck.com

Like us on Facebook @ Moments With Yahweh

Visit our website: mwy4chuck.com

Cover by Tajul Ahamed

DEDICATION

To Zeny and Bell

You have been by my side since the beginning of this journey. I could not do this without the love and support you both have freely given.

ACKNOWLEDGMENTS

No book is written by one individual, it takes a small army to bring a concept to publication. I hope I have included everyone involved in this project. If I have missed anyone, please forgive me. First and foremost is my Proverbs 31 wife, Zeny, who has stood beside me as I struggled to write from behind my carefully crafted walls, and who painstakingly worked behind the scenes to bring this book to life. Bell, our teenage daughter who put up with my need for silence. Your patience is amazing! Allan my brother from another mother and who knows me better than I know myself. Jackie, Allan's best friend, confident, and spouse – thank you for always being willing to share my brother with me. Philana, who challenged me to take my creative writing skills and use them for the LORD. Daryl and Kelvin, my accountability partners who have been involved in talking through all phases of this book and gently redirecting my stubborn mindset. Pastors Cleve Smith and Scott Wiles who are gracious with their time and always willing to discuss theological points. Chris, Charity, Shanda, and Trina for believing in me. Brooke, who has walked with me through every stage of this book as well as providing some of her own devotionals. The Just Digging Deeper small group at Calvary Community Church who constantly encourage me. Most importantly I want to thank my LORD and Savior Jesus Christ, who died that I might live. You left this earth to sit at the right hand of the Father, making way for the Holy Spirit who has given me a tremendous spiritual gift and talents galore to go along with it.

FORWARD

When we were first dating Allan would look at an incoming call and say "I've got to take this…" and abruptly step out. At first, I was confused about why this individual had so much influence on my man. But after learning more about Chuck, it made perfect sense. I have been privy to a few of my husband's chats with Chuck on the phone. Those conversations are extremely insightful and have had a powerful impact on Allan spiritually and otherwise. In fact, one profound question he asked when Allan made the call to let Chuck know he was asking me to marry him was, "When Jackie corrects you, are you open to what she is saying, or do you get defensive?"

We are in our 6th year of marriage as I write this, and it never fails that our family has a complex theological discussion, and a "we should ask Chuck his thoughts on this" comes up. I take great comfort in knowing Chuck is a phone call away for Allan as he always comes away refreshed when hanging up. I have used Chuck's first book "A Refreshing Chuckle" in my women's small group. It is a fabulous option as many attendees don't do the homework in other book studies. This has been instrumental in creating an inclusive environment for new participants. The topics apply to everyday life. The questions challenge you deeper into community and into the Word. I am excited about this second book. We are honored to hold a piece of Chuck's wisdom and teaching to live on in print so that we can share it with those we love.

Jackie Roche
President
Jackie's Natural Cleaning Inc.
Salem, Oregon

Allan:

Wait a minute! "Dr. Chuck Glenn"? Okay, that just doesn't sit right with me, it just seems so strange… "Dr. Chuck Glenn". Why does it seem so strange? He's my brother from another set of parents. If you doubt this ask Chuck about the time mom had to throw us out of the house because we were two grown men engaged in a wrestling match that started in her den and ended when we progressed through the house to her "living room." (I don't know why we decided to have a wrestling match, but when we wrestled our way into the living room there was an abundance of living going on.)

When Chuck and I first met it was while opening a new store as department managers. I oversaw electronics while Chuck oversaw computers and appliances. Between the two of us, we knew that for the store to succeed we both had to exceed our goals. I manage as a drill sergeant: "Here's what needs to be done now do it!". Chuck, on the other hand: "Here's what needs to be done. Let me tell you why this is good for you. Next let me teach you how to get there… and remember I will be here with you to help you along the way…"

When a person leans into Chuck for support, he listens carefully and then brings up a scripture that is perfect for the situation. He doesn't just quote the scripture; he takes time to explain why it is relevant to the situation and how it can be incorporated into one's life. He also lets the person know that he is there to help as one walks through the issue they have discussed. Sound familiar?

One of Chuck's favorite chapters in the Bible is Romans Chapter 6, which he has memorized. I've lost count of how many times Chuck has quoted the first four verses of this chapter whenever someone brings up the guilt he is experiencing due to the hold sin has on his life. Chuck emphasizes that in our new life in Christ, we are created to walk with Him. Therefore, it's natural that when we do something conflicting with our new life, we feel guilty. Here are the first four verses of Romans Chapter 6.

"(1) What shall we say then? Are we to continue in sin that grace may abound? (2) By no means! How can we who died to sin still live in it? (3) Do you not know that all of us who have been baptized into Christ Jesus were baptized into his death? (4) We were buried therefore with him by baptism into death, in order that, just as Christ was raised from the dead by the glory of the Father, we too might walk in newness of life." (English Standard Version)

He also points out that 1 John 1:8-9 tells us that everyone sins and that through asking for forgiveness all our sins are cleansed. His favorite question to ask after quoting 1 John 1:8-9 is "What do you think the word 'all' means?"

Another one of Chuck's favorite verses is Philippians 4:6 "Do not be anxious about anything, but in everything by prayer and supplication with thanksgiving let your requests be made known to God." When individuals come to Chuck about their anxiety, he listens, quotes this verse, and urges them to make it a part of their daily lives. He also lets them know he will be praying with them. Whenever I get a call from Chuck saying, "I want to ask you something," or "I need to talk about something," I know it is because he is anxious and needs to be reminded to pray. So I have this verse locked and loaded... It always applies. ALWAYS. I give him the same short answer I give everyone; this verse means don't WORRY about ANYTHING! Take EVERYTHING to GOD in prayer with a thankful heart. Chuck listens and thanks me for reminding him of what he needs to do.

A Refreshing Chuckle II is designed for someone like me who is a light reader. The puns draw you in, in a great way, to open up your thinking. It's ironic that "Mr. what words mean based on how they are spoken, where they are spoken, and when they were spoken" would use puns with double word meanings to explore perspectives of God's Word. Chuck's life has been a never-ending pursuit of God. His drive for not just knowing God's word but understanding the meaning of the words based on the time, place, and people involved when it was written is relentless. This has given him an in-depth understanding of who God is and Who God has been to all of His people throughout time.

Allan Roche
Secretary
Jackie's Natural Cleaning Inc.
Salem, Oregon

TABLE OF CONTENTS

TABLE OF CONTENTS

RECEDING HARE LINE

What do you call a line of rabbits marching backward?

A receding Hare line!

Have you ever felt like you're marching backward in your faith journey? Maybe you've taken steps away from God, and you're not sure how to turn things around. It can be discouraging to feel like you're moving away from the one who loves you most.

But take heart! The Bible reminds us that God knows us intimately, even when we feel like we're hiding in the shadows. Psalm 51:6 says, "Behold, You desire truth in the innermost being, and in the hidden part You will make me know wisdom."

God desires truth in our innermost being, that means He knows our hearts, even when we try to hide our thoughts and feelings. And in those hidden places, He can reveal wisdom to us that we might not have discovered otherwise. So even when we feel like we're marching in a "receding hare line" away from God, we can trust that He still sees us and knows us. But how do we turn things around when we've strayed from God's path?

The good news is that we can always come back to Him, no matter how far we've gone. In fact, He is waiting for us with open arms, ready to welcome us home. Psalm 51:10-12 gives us a beautiful prayer for repentance and renewal: "Create in me a clean heart, O God, And renew a steadfast spirit within me. Do not cast me away from Your presence And do not take Your Holy Spirit from me. Restore to me the joy of Your salvation And sustain me with a willing spirit."

Let these words be a guide for you as you seek to return to God. Ask Him to create in you a clean heart and renew your spirit, so that you can be steadfast in your faith. Ask Him to restore the joy of your salvation, and to sustain you with a willing spirit.

Remember, God loves you and wants you to come back to Him. No matter how far you've strayed, He is always ready to welcome you home with open arms. So don't be discouraged by a "receding Hare line," instead, turn to God and let Him lead you forward on your faith journey.

NOTES:

_____

_____

_____

_____

_____

_____

_____

_____

_____

_____

_____

_____

CARNIVAL WORKERS

How do you regain control of panicked carnival workers?
You go for the juggler

That's a funny pun, but it also has a deeper meaning. When we feel like we're losing control, it's often because we're being attacked at our core. Our jugular represents the vulnerable parts of us that, when threatened, can cause us to panic.

In Matthew 11:29, Jesus offers us a solution to this problem. He says, "Take my yoke upon you and learn from Me, for I am gentle and humble in heart, and YOU WILL FIND REST FOR YOUR SOULS." When we feel like we're losing control, we can turn to Jesus and find rest for our souls.

But what does it mean to take Jesus' yoke upon us? It means submitting to His will and His ways, instead of trying to do things our own way. When we try to do things our own way, we often end up making mistakes that leave us feeling vulnerable and exposed. But when we follow Jesus' way, we can find the rest and peace that our souls need.

So how does Jesus help us when we feel like we're losing control? First, He calls us to repent. When we've made mistakes, it's important to acknowledge them and ask for forgiveness. This can be a humbling experience, but it's also a necessary one. Additionally, Jesus shows us through His word what we did wrong. The Bible is full of wisdom and guidance that can help us navigate life's challenges. When we turn to the Bible for guidance, we can find the answers we need to regain control. Finally, Jesus explains how not to make the same mistakes again. He offers us His grace and His love, and He empowers us to live according to His will. When we follow His way, we can avoid the pitfalls that often leave us feeling vulnerable and exposed.

In the end, Jesus doesn't attack us like a carnival worker going for the juggler. Instead, He embraces us with His love and His grace. He sends us back into the game of life with a supportive pat on the back, knowing that we have everything we need to succeed.

So if you're feeling like you're losing control, remember Jesus' words in Matthew 11:29. Take His yoke upon you, learn from Him, and find rest for your soul. When you do, you'll be amazed at how much easier life can be.

NOTES:

_____

_____

_____

_____

_____

_____

_____

_____

_____

_____

_____

_____

_____

_____

_____

_____

TIRED ARMY

Why was King Arthur's army too tired to fight?
It had too many sleepless knights.

I remember a night when I was sleepless. My wife worked a shift from two to ten p.m. It was typical for her to stay over at work for thirty minutes or so, but this night, in the middle of a blizzard, midnight rolled around and she was not home. As a nurse, she wasn't allowed to have her cell phone on the floor with her. Neither was she allowed to receive or make personal calls. As I lay on the couch waiting for the sound of her tires crunching on the frozen snow outside, I found myself pleading for God to protect her and get her home safely, which He did.

I have found that being sleepless because of anxiety is a common trait among my friends and family. However, there is another situation when I am sleepless and it has nothing to do with worry. During these times I've learned to say "LORD what should I be praying for?" One time He told me to pray for the inmates by name in the prison I served as a Religious Coordinator (Chaplin). I spent the rest of that night and the next several nights praying through every name on each housing unit's roster. When I was finished the prison roster, I had peace. As I questioned praying for men I knew nothing about, The LORD brought 1 Timothy 2:1 to my mind. "First of all, then, I urge that entreaties and prayers, petitions and thanksgivings, be made on behalf of all men."

The next time you are sleepless during the night, quietly ask God who or what He wants you to pray for. As you begin praying, you will find God's peace taking over.

NOTES:

5

RUNNING OUT OF PATIENCE
B.L. Glenn

Why did the Squid go to the office supply store?
It ran out of ink!.

Running out of something can be inconvenient, whether it's milk and eggs or the gas in your car. Here in America, we usually solve a low-supply situation with ease: go to the store for food or go to the gas station for gas, and presto! Problem solved.

But what about running out of things that run along the intangible, like love or patience? Abraham struggled with patience when he lay awake in his tent, worrying over how the Lord would bring him a son through Sarah. Moses lost his temper and struck the rock in the wilderness of Sinai after 40 years of leading a group of people who did nothing but constantly complain when they were brought out of Egypt. However, I cannot point a finger in accusation at them because I have found that oftentimes I run out of patience in the seasons of persistent-yet-unanswered prayer.

It is at times like this that Christ brings His word to the front of my mind. Romans 5:3-5 says, "And not only this, but we also exult in our tribulations, knowing that tribulation brings about perseverance; and perseverance, proven character; and proven character, hope; and hope does not disappoint, because the love of God has been poured out within our hearts through the Holy Spirit who was given to us.

I can't help but marvel at how suffering and hope are woven together in this passage. Suffering comes from trials. But as we follow Paul's line of reasoning in these verses, we see that suffering leads to hope and hope makes us not ashamed because God pours his love (Godly love) into us through the Holy Spirit. In the Greek language "poured out" means to bestow liberally.

How God stands ready to pour out His love! If you are struggling with a loss of patience, dear friend, look to the One who has poured out His love in you and trust Him for a deeper awareness of it! He will come and will not delay.

NOTES:

_____

_____

_____

_____

_____

_____

_____

_____

_____

_____

_____

_____

_____

_____

_____

_____

_____

_____

_____

_____

CIRCUS FIRE

Did you hear about the Circus Fire?
It was in tents.

There have been times in my life that have been intense, like the first time I experienced rappelling. Somehow, walking backward over the side of a cliff with the ground 100 feet below, hooked up to a rope threaded through an object shaped like a "D," and with no safety net below me, just did not make sense. Thankfully I had an experienced person by my side. He went first and had the nerve to tell me to look over the cliff. When I peeked over, I saw a couple of specks at the bottom of the cliff which seemed to be attached to the end of each of our ropes.

My rappelling buddy looked at me with a gleam in his eye and said, "Watch this." He then bent his knees, pushed off the cliff, and let go with both hands while yelling "falling!" The speck at the end of his rope immediately turned into the rope, faced away from the cliff, and started to run. The result was that the rope stretched tight and my buddy's fall was suspended. He just hung there, safely in midair. He smiled at me and said, "Believe in the person on the end of the rope, he will take care of you."

When I face intense times in my life (loss of job, stressful situations at work, etc.) I need to remember to believe in the person who is at the end of my rope. Jesus said in John 14:1 "Do not let your heart be troubled, believe in God, believe also in Me." That verse tells me that Jesus is at the end of my rope. He tells me to believe in Him and He will keep me safe.

NOTES:

_____

_____

_____

DUCK, EGGS
B.L. Glenn

I passed a farm with a sign posted out front: "Duck, eggs." I said, "That's an unnecessary comma…"
Then it hit me.

I've never been hit by an egg. But I remember a time that I was hit out of nowhere by the love of God.

I had been in charge of a big project with my classmates at college. The project went off well, but I made a mess of the process and hurt a lot of people. It was a Saturday night, the night after our project was finished. Our campus was strangely empty. I was wandering around the grounds, depressed and listless. I was extra aware of my failings and how poorly I had led my team.

I wandered to the fields in front of the dorms, just a long stretch of grass and hill when it hit me. Or should I say, when He hit me? It was like I was ambushed by the love of God. I was strongly aware of His kindness, affection, and sweetness. I felt like I was drowning in an ocean of it. The yawning cavern of my failings became only shadows that accentuated His glory. I was suddenly swept up by this Being who knows my frame and remembers that I am dust. And yet, who loves me with everlasting love.

I have never been more acutely aware of the LORD than I was that night. He doesn't send moments like that very often, but when He does, watch out! He can sweep you off your feet before you know what's coming.

In his prayer for the Ephesians (Ephesians 3:14-19), Paul sought for the eyes of their hearts to be enlightened, and for them to be strengthened to grasp the immense depth, width, and height of God's love—a love that surpasses all knowledge. I find it fascinating Paul prays that God would give them *strength* to comprehend Christ's love. It's as though Paul knows that the love

9

of God is too strong a thought, too overflowing, too deep and wide for our human hearts to grasp. He longs for the Church to understand this love on a deeper level.

I don't know about you, but I feel love strongest when it is shown at a time that I least deserve it. What has your past week or month been like? Have you fallen short of your resolve?

NOTES:

_____

_____

_____

_____

_____

_____

_____

_____

_____

_____

_____

_____

_____

_____

_____

_____

_____

_____

_____

COMMUNICATING TURTLES

How do turtles communicate with each other?
With shell phones!

Every time I read that pun; I think it is just plain silly. Shell phones? Really? Of course, what makes it funny are the words shell phones instead of cell phones. What is interesting is that when we use cell phones to communicate, we cannot see, feel or smell the person we are talking to. I have met people who will not communicate with anyone unless they see them face to face. That's what some people think when they hear Christians speak about talking to God. They believe that talking to God is nothing more than speaking words to some unknown "thing" way out in the Universe (if they even acknowledge that there is "thing" way out in the Universe).

When a person tells me that talking to God is crazy because He cannot see, physically feel, or smell God, I agree. I tell him that talking and communicating with a being whom we cannot see hear or smell seems crazy. But then I ask if the person has ever smelled the freshness of the rain. I ask him if he knows where that smell comes from. Then I point out Romans 1:20 "For since the creation of the world His invisible attributes, His eternal power, and divine nature, have been clearly seen, being understood through what has been made…" Next, I move to the issue of knowing the presence of something unseen. I ask the person if he has ever felt afraid. When I receive a positive answer (all of us have experienced being afraid) I tell him that just like he can feel fear although it is unseen, we can also feel God. God may be unseen but He is a very real presence. I point out that all of us feel happiness, love, and comfort even though we can't see them. Then I share how God's comfort is different than anything I have ever felt or experienced.

11

At this point, I turn to Proverbs 3:5-6. I point out that God tells us to trust in Him with all our souls and acknowledge Him in all our ways. When we do that, He will make our paths straight. I also point out that God cannot make a person's path straight if the person does not acknowledge His existence. The fact is that He cannot guide us unless we speak to Him. Jeremiah 42:3 says, "Pray that the LORD your God may tell us the way we should walk and the thing we should do." God's promise is this: if we talk to Him He will direct us in the way we should go.

NOTES:

_____

_____

_____

_____

_____

_____

_____

_____

_____

_____

_____

_____

_____

_____

_____

_____

_____

LOST ELECTRON

I am positive I just lost an electron.
Better keep an ion that.

That may sound like a silly joke, but it has a spiritual application. In 1 Corinthians 6:9-10, Paul lists several sins that will keep people from inheriting the kingdom of God. It's a daunting list, and if we stopped reading there, we might feel discouraged and hopeless. But thankfully, the passage doesn't end there. Verse 11 provides a powerful reminder that we are not defined by our past mistakes: "Such were some of you; but you were washed, but you were sanctified, but you were justified in the name of the Lord Jesus Christ and in the Spirit of our God."

Notice the past tense in that verse. It doesn't say "such *are* some of you," as if those sins still define who we are. Instead, it says "such *were,* (italics and underline mine), some of you." In Christ, we are new creations (2 Corinthians 5:17), and our old selves have been crucified with him (Romans 6:6).

So when we feel weighed down by guilt and shame over our past sins, we can remember that we have been washed clean by the blood of Jesus. We have been sanctified, set apart for God's purposes, and we have been justified, declared righteous in God's sight. This is not something we earned or achieved on our own; it is a gift of grace that we received through faith in Jesus.

And just like the pun reminds us to keep an ion (eye on) what we have, we can also keep our focus on Jesus and His saving work in our lives. When we fix our eyes on Him, we can find hope and strength to resist temptation and live in a way that pleases God.

The next time you hear a pun about electrons and ions, remember that it's not just a silly joke. It's a reminder that in Christ, we have been transformed and made new. We can leave our past sins behind and live with confidence in the grace and mercy of our Savior.

NOTES:

_____

_____

_____

_____

_____

_____

_____

_____

_____

_____

_____

_____

_____

_____

_____

_____

_____

_____

_____

A NERVOUS WRECK

What lies at the bottom of the ocean and twitches?
A nervous wreck.

As a Christian, I know I'm not supposed to be a nervous wreck, but the truth is, I often am. Sometimes, the smallest things can set me off. For example, when my family isn't home when I expect them to be, or when I have to give a presentation, or even when I'm playing golf and worrying about where my ball will end up.

When I start feeling anxious, it's easy to quote Philippians 4:6: "Be anxious for nothing, but in everything by prayer and supplication with thanksgiving let your requests be made known to God." But actually living out that scripture is a whole different story. That's why I find comfort in Psalm 3, where David prays and lies down to sleep, but then comes back to God asking for help. If a man after God's own heart had to keep bringing his worries to God, then it's okay for me to do the same.

When I look at Philippians 4:6 more closely, I notice that there's no limit on what we can bring before God. We're instructed to bring everything to Him, so even if I've already prayed about something, it's okay to bring it up again if I'm still feeling anxious. Another verse that helps me with anxiety is Isaiah 41:10: "Do not fear, for I am with you; Do not anxiously look about you, for I am your God. I will strengthen you, surely I will help you, Surely I will uphold you with My righteous right hand." When I remember that God is always with me, ready to strengthen, help, and uphold me, it gives me the courage to face whatever is causing my anxiety.

If you're feeling like a nervous wreck today, remember that you're not alone. Bring your worries before God, even if you've already done so before, and trust that He will give you the strength and help you need. Always remember, that as a child of God, you have access to His peace that surpasses all understanding (Philippians 4:7).

Take a moment to breathe deeply and rest in His presence. Let His peace fill your heart and mind, and trust that He is in control of all things. Remember, anxiety may come, but it doesn't have to rule over you. With God's help, you can overcome it and live a life of peace and joy.

NOTES:

_____

_____

_____

_____

_____

_____

_____

_____

_____

_____

_____

_____

_____

_____

_____

_____

SEMI-COLON

What happened when the semi-colon broke grammar laws?

He was given two consecutive sentences..

Have you ever felt like you've broken the rules, like you've messed up so badly that there's no going back? Maybe you've made a mistake at work or said something hurtful to a friend. Maybe you've even broken a law and found yourself in trouble with the authorities.

When we break the rules, there are usually consequences. We might lose our job, damage a relationship, or face legal penalties. And if we're honest with ourselves, we know that we deserve those consequences. We know that we were wrong and that we need to make things right.

But here's the amazing thing about God's grace: even when we break the rules, even when we deserve punishment, He still offers us forgiveness and a chance to start over. In fact, He offers us not just one chance, but consecutive sentences. What do I mean by consecutive sentences? Well, in grammar, a sentence is a complete thought expressed in words. And when we use a semicolon to join two related sentences, we create a connection between them that goes beyond what a period or a comma could do. The two sentences become one, with a new meaning that is greater than the sum of its parts.

In the same way, when we turn to God for forgiveness, He doesn't just forgive us and leave us to our own devices. He offers us a new life, a new purpose, a new direction. He gives us not just one chance to start over, but multiple chances as well. You see, God forgives and forgets our sins when we confess them to Him (Isaiah 43:25 and 1 John 1:9).

17

This means God gives us unlimited chances when we approach Him with a broken and shattered heart asking for forgiveness.

So if you're feeling like you've broken the rules and there's no going back, remember that God's grace is greater than your mistakes. He always forgives and always provides another chance to make things right. All you have to do is ask for forgiveness and trust in His love.

Let's pray: Dear God, thank you for your amazing grace that offers us forgiveness and a second chance. Help us to trust in your love and to live our lives in a way that honors you. Amen.

NOTES:

_____

_____

_____

_____

_____

_____

_____

_____

_____

_____

_____

_____

_____

RUFFING THE PASSER

Why did the dog get called for a penalty at the football game?
He was ruffing the passer.

Have you ever been clueless about something, just like a dog at a football game? Maybe it's something you're struggling to understand, like a difficult concept at work or a complex relationship. Or perhaps it's something bigger, like your purpose in life or your relationship with God.

When we're clueless, it's easy to try to rely on our own understanding. We might think we have it all figured out, or we might try to Google our way to a solution. But the truth is, our own understanding is limited. Just like a dog can't understand the rules of football, we can't understand everything on our own.

So what should we do when we're clueless? Proverbs 3:5-6 gives us the answer: "Trust in the LORD with all your heart and do not lean on your own understanding. In all your ways acknowledge Him, and He will make your paths straight." This verse reminds us that we don't have to rely on our own understanding. Instead, we can trust in the LORD. We can acknowledge Him in all our ways, and He will guide us on the right path. It's a promise we can hold onto, no matter how clueless we might feel.

But what does it mean to trust in the LORD? It means putting our faith in Him, even when we don't understand what's going on. It means surrendering our own plans and desires, and seeking His will instead. It means listening for His voice, and following His lead. Trusting in the LORD isn't always easy. Sometimes it requires us to step out of our comfort zones, or to wait patiently for His timing. But when we do trust in Him, we can have confidence that He will make our paths straight. He will guide us

19

to where we need to be, even if we don't fully understand the journey.

The next time you're feeling clueless, remember the dog at the football game. Instead of trying to figure it out on your own, trust in the LORD. Lean on Him, acknowledge Him, and let Him guide you on the right path. And who knows, maybe you'll even be able to avoid a penalty for "ruffing the passer!"

NOTES:

_____

_____

_____

_____

_____

_____

_____

_____

_____

_____

_____

_____

_____

_____

_____

HOW DAIRY

A man just assaulted me with milk, cream, and butter.
How dairy.

Have you ever had someone do something to you that made you want to scream, cry, or even fight back? It's easy to get caught up in our emotions and react impulsively when we feel wronged. But as the wise grandfather in the Native American story said, there are two wolves inside each of us, one angry and full of rage, and the other calm and peaceful. The one that wins the fight is the one we feed the most.

So how do we feed the peaceful wolf when someone has just assaulted us with milk, cream, and butter? First, let's take a moment to appreciate the humor in the situation. It's not every day that we get attacked by dairy products! Sometimes, finding the humor in a difficult situation can help us step back from our emotions and see things from a different perspective.

But beyond the humor, there's a deeper lesson here. In Proverbs 10, we see a list of negative actions we should avoid, such as spreading lies or stirring up conflict. These actions feed the raging wolf inside of us and lead to more anger and frustration. But for each negative action, there's a positive one we can do. We can speak words of wisdom, seek peace, and show love. These actions feed the peaceful wolf and bring us closer to God.

When someone does something hurtful or frustrating, we have a choice. We can give in to our anger and feed the raging wolf, or we can choose to respond with wisdom and love, feeding the peaceful wolf instead. It's not always easy, but with God's help, we can overcome our natural instincts and choose to do what's right.

As we go about our day, let's remember the two wolves inside of us and choose to feed the one that brings us closer to God. And the next time someone assaults us with milk, cream, and butter, let's choose to find the humor in the situation and respond with love instead of anger. After all, how dairy!

NOTES:

_____

_____

_____

_____

_____

_____

_____

_____

_____

_____

_____

_____

_____

_____

_____

_____

_____

_____

_____

HOT DOG'S HAIRDO

What is a hot dog's favorite hairdo?
A Bun!

What is a hot dog's favorite hairdo? A Bun! While this pun might make you smile, it can also teach us a valuable lesson about temptation. Just as a hot dog needs a bun to hold it together, our souls need the right "bun" to protect us from temptation and keep us on the right path.

In 2 Timothy 2:22, Paul gives us a simple but powerful temptation chart to follow: "Run from anything that stimulates youthful lusts. Instead, pursue righteous living, faithfulness, love, and peace. Enjoy the companionship of those who call on the Lord with pure hearts." (NLT) This verse reminds us that we must be intentional about avoiding anything that could lead us astray, and instead focus on living a life that pleases God. But what exactly does "anything" mean in this context? It means anything that tempts us to sin or gives into our sinful desires. This could be anything from watching inappropriate content, to gossiping about others, or even over-indulging in food or alcohol. Whatever it may be, we must be willing to recognize it and run from it, just as we would run from a bad hot dog that could make us sick.

It's important to note that avoiding temptation doesn't mean we have to live in isolation or avoid all forms of pleasure. Rather, we should focus on pursuing righteous living, faithfulness, love, and peace, as Paul instructs. We should surround ourselves with friends and companions who share our values and encourage us to grow closer to God.

The next time you're faced with temptation, remember to ask yourself: What is my "bun" for the soul? What can I rely on to protect me and keep me on the right path? And always remember,

God is with you every step of the way, ready to help you overcome any temptation that comes your way.

NOTES:

_____

_____

_____

_____

_____

_____

_____

_____

_____

_____

_____

_____

_____

_____

_____

_____

_____

_____

_____

THE PAWS BUTTON

How does a lion stop a video?
He hits the paws button.

Have you ever felt overwhelmed by the demands of life? Maybe it's work, family, relationships, or just the busyness of everyday living. It's easy to get caught up in the hustle and bustle and forget to take a moment to rest. In the midst of our fast-paced world, God invites us to hit the paws button. Yes, you read that right - the "paws" button. Just like a lion stopping a video, we too can take a break and pause for a moment.

But why is it so important to pause? When we take a step back, we allow ourselves to recharge and refocus. We give ourselves the space to connect with God and hear His voice. It's in these moments of rest that we find peace, clarity, and renewed strength. The psalmist reminds us to "cease striving and know that [God] is God." (Psalm 46:10) When we stop trying to do everything on our own, we recognize that God is in control. He is the one who sustains us and gives us the ability to carry on.

How do we hit the pause button? It can look different for everyone. Maybe it's taking a few deep breaths, going for a walk, or simply sitting in silence. Whatever it may be, it's essential to make rest a priority in our lives. As we hit the pause button and rest, we can trust that God is at work. He is the one who fights our battles and carries our burdens. We don't have to strive or worry because He has already gone before us and prepared the way.

In Matthew 11:28-30, Jesus says, "Come to me, all who are weary and heavy-laden, and I will give you rest. Take my yoke upon you and learn from Me, for I am gentle and humble in heart, and YOU WILL FIND REST FOR YOUR SOULS. For my yoke is easy and my burden is light." As we seek rest in God, we can find true peace and refreshment.

So, the next time you feel overwhelmed, remember to hit the pause button and rest in God's loving embrace.

Prayer:

Dear God, thank you for inviting us to rest in you. Help us to hit the pause button and find true peace in your presence. Give us the strength to lay down our burdens and trust in your sovereignty. May we find refreshment and renewal as we seek rest in you. In Jesus' name, amen.

NOTES:

_____

_____

_____

_____

_____

_____

_____

_____

_____

_____

_____

_____

_____

_____

_____

HOKEY POKEY

I was addicted to the hokey-pokey.
Thankfully I turned myself around.

Have you ever heard the phrase "you can't save yourself"? It's a concept that is central to Christianity, and it's one that can be difficult to grasp. We like to think that we can pull ourselves up by our own bootstraps, that we can fix our own problems, and that we can earn our own salvation. But the truth is, we can't. We are all addicted to something, whether it's a substance, a behavior, or even our own self-righteousness. And we can't turn ourselves around on our own.

But here's the good news: we don't have to. In Titus 3:5, we read that "He saved us, not on the basis of deeds which we have done in righteousness, but according to His mercy…" It's not about what we do, it's about what He has done for us. We don't have to be perfect; we don't have to clean ourselves up, and we don't have to earn His love. It's freely given to us, and all we have to do is accept it.

Now, let's get back to that pun: "I was addicted to the hokey pokey. Thankfully I turned myself around." It's a lighthearted way to describe a serious truth. We all have areas in our lives that require transformation, whether it involves overcoming an addiction, abandoning detrimental habits, or shifting towards a more positive mindset. But going it alone isn't the solution. We need the help of a Savior who loves us unconditionally and who has already done the work for us.

If you're feeling like you need to turn yourself around before you can be good enough for God, remember this: it's not about you. It's about Him. His righteousness covers our sins, and His grace is sufficient for us. We don't have to clean ourselves up before we come to Him. We can come to Him just as we are, with all our flaws and imperfections, and He will still love us.

Let's all take a moment to reflect on our own lives and ask ourselves what we need to turn around. But let's also remember that we can't do it on our own. We need the help of a loving Savior who has already done the work for us. And let's give thanks for His mercy and grace, which are freely given to us.

NOTES:

_____

_____

_____

_____

_____

_____

_____

_____

_____

_____

_____

_____

_____

_____

_____

_____

_____

TIRED MOTORCYCLES
B.L. Glenn

Why can't motorcycles hold themselves up?
Because they are two-tired.

Have you ever been so tired that you have trouble holding yourself up? I certainly have. One particularly grueling experience comes to mind: My friend and I had decided to take two weeks each year and hike the Appalachian trail in sections. The farther we worked our way north, the steeper the mountains became. We would pitch camp for the night, unfold our map over a re-hydrated bag of beans and rice, and plan our hike for the next day. This particular year, both of us had led more sedentary lives than previously…and we felt it! About five days into our trip we saw that a hostel was only twelve miles away and that the hike to get there would be mostly downhill. We were ecstatic. Twelve miles downhill and a warm bed at the end of it? Yes, please!

Things did not turn out as expected. The hike that next day was demanding: every muscle was tense, every part of the path was difficult. It *was* downhill, but the downhill consisted of climbing down boulders. Every single one of those twelve miles demanded constant vigilance and attention. The trail wearied our minds because every move was calculated (if you missed a foothold on one of the boulders while wearing a heavy pack, the momentum caused by the shifting of your pack placed you at risk of falling into whatever ravine that boulder guarded). By mid-afternoon, our bodies were stiff with burning muscles and we were struggling to put one foot in front of the other. I weakly suggested that we stop for the night at the covered shelter that had been built just off the trail, a mile from our intended destination, but my friend was determined to have an actual bed. We hiked on.

The sun was settling into dusk as we finally dragged ourselves into the hostel. Everything was closed. The restaurant. The front desk. Even when we managed to find a staff and convince them to rent us a room, we were disappointed. The warm beds we dreamed of turned out to be hard uncomfortable bunks. That night, every time I moved, I woke up because of the burning in my muscles. Every time I woke, my dog whined and wagged her tail…hoping, I think, that I would massage her aching body a bit before we drifted off into a fitful sleep again. Nothing has ever compared to the fatigue we all felt that day.

Sometimes life is like that. There are stretches of life where we may have expected it to be easy, but lo and behold, we find that we must exercise every ounce of trust and perseverance to get through it. Sometimes they come when we feel like we are already at the end of our strength. Sometimes the season lasts for years.

When life gets dark and difficult, where can a person turn? To the One who carries us on eagle's wings and brings us to Himself. Asaph, in Psalm 73:23-24, 26 says this: "Nevertheless, I am continually with You; You have taken hold of my right hand. With Your counsel you will guide me, and afterward, receive me to your glory. My heart and my flesh may fail, but God is the strength of my heart and my portion forever…." When we are struggling to put one foot in front of the other, we need to turn to Him, let Him take our hand, and give us strength.

I am confident of one thing. He does not have an uncomfortable bunk waiting for us at the end of this. No, He has gone to prepare a room for us in His house. One day, He will bring us there. When we arrive, all of those boulders, all of the aches and pains, all of the long days and sleepless nights, will be nothing compared with the glory He has prepared for us.

NOTES:

BASKETBALL PLAYERS ON VACATION
B.L. Glenn

Why don't basketball players go on vacation?
Because they aren't allowed to travel.

I can imagine that if anyone felt like going on a vacation, it was the disciples when they were returning from preaching in the towns and villages. In Mark 6:7-13 we read that Jesus sent them out in pairs after giving them authority over unclean spirits and authorizing them to anoint sick people with oil and heal them. When they returned, Jesus called them and said "…Come away by yourselves to a secluded place and rest a little while…" (Mark 6:30). Jesus' thought was to give His disciples a rest after their intense time of ministry. The crowds, however, had another idea.

The miracles and teachings given by Christ and His disciples were too great to pass up, and the crowds followed them to their vacation spot. However, instead of rebuking the crowds and turning them away with a sharp word, Jesus stood up and taught them. He taught for a long time, so long that it was getting too late to send them away to get food in the nearest village. When the disciples pointed this out to Him, Jesus said, "…You give them something to eat…" (Mark 6:37).

We know, from this story, that there were at least 5,000 men there. That number does not include women and children. We can safely assume there were at least 15,000 mouths to feed, and that's a conservative number! While some of the disciples were exclaiming that there wasn't enough money in a year's wages to feed all of these people, Andrew was busy talking to a little boy who had thought to bring his lunch along. The boy offered his lunch to Andrew, who brought it to Jesus. Jesus prayed over it and broke it up into twelve baskets, and the rest is history. Thousands of people ate as much as they wanted, and there were twelve baskets left over

There was a crisis: "How can this crowd be fed?" There was a small offering, "What about this bread and fish?" And there was an act of God on their behalf, "Everyone ate their fill…"

Sometimes, when we most want a vacation from the chaos in our lives, when we have been going and going for a long while and feel like we cannot go much longer, we can be asked to give above and beyond what we are able. It is in this choice point, this stretching of our capacities past our human limitations, that the Lord can come and work wonders.

NOTES:

_____

_____

_____

_____

_____

_____

_____

_____

_____

_____

_____

_____

_____

_____

SLEEPLESS KNIGHTS

Why was king Arthur's army too tired to fight?
All those sleepless knights!

Have you ever felt like you've been facing difficult challenges that have drained your energy and left you feeling exhausted? Perhaps you're struggling with anxiety, depression, or other mental health issues that make it hard for you to sleep or find rest. Whatever your situation may be, take heart and be encouraged, for the LORD is with you.

In Psalm 121:1-8, the psalmist declares: "I will lift up my eyes to the mountains; from where shall my help come? My help comes from the LORD, who made heaven and earth. He will not allow your foot to slip; He who keeps you will not slumber. Behold, He who keeps Israel will neither slumber nor sleep. The LORD is your keeper; the LORD is your shade on your right hand. The sun will not smite you by day, nor the moon by night. The LORD will protect you from all evil; He will keep your soul. The LORD will guard your going out and your coming in from this time forth and forever."

This psalm reminds us that God is always watching over us, even when we're too tired to fight or too sleepless to rest. He is our helper, our keeper, our protector, and our guard. He never slumbers or sleeps, so we can always trust Him to be there for us, day or night. When we feel overwhelmed or exhausted, we can turn to God in prayer and ask Him for strength, courage, and peace. He promises that His Holy Spirit, already within us, will empower us to overcome every obstacle and fight every battle.

In Galatians 5:22-23, the apostle Paul describes the fruits of the Holy Spirit: "But the fruit of the Spirit is love, joy, peace, patience, kindness, goodness, faithfulness, gentleness, self-control; against such things there is no law." These fruits are not something we can produce on our own, but they are the result of the Holy Spirit working in us and through us.

If you're feeling too tired to fight, ask God for the fruits of the Holy Spirit. Ask Him to fill you with His love, joy, peace, patience, kindness, goodness, faithfulness, gentleness, and self-control. Ask Him to help you rest in Him, to trust Him with your battles, and to rely on His strength instead of your own. Remember, you are not alone in your struggles.

So take heart, and be encouraged. Even when you're surrounded by sleepless nights, you can find rest in the LORD. He is your help, your keeper, your shade, your protector, and your guard. Trust in Him, and He will give you the strength to fight on.

NOTES:

_____

_____

_____

_____

_____

_____

_____

_____

_____

_____

_____

_____

_____

_____

WHAT ISSUES

During the COVID outbreak, they said we could gather
with up to eight people without issues.
I don't know eight people without issues.

During the COVID outbreak, we were told that we could gather
with up to eight people without issues. But let's be honest, how
many of us can say that we know eight people without issues? We
all have our struggles, and sometimes it can be hard to open up
and share our innermost thoughts and feelings with others. We
worry that we might be burdening them or that they won't
understand what we're going through.

However, as Christians, we are called to bear one another's
burdens and to encourage one another. But how can we do this if
we don't feel comfortable sharing our own struggles? The answer
can be found in Philippians 4:6, which says, "Be anxious for
nothing, but in everything by prayer and supplication with
thanksgiving let your requests be made known to God."

God knows everything about us, including our innermost
thoughts and feelings. He knows the burdens we carry and the
struggles we face. And the best part is, He wants us to bring our
concerns to Him. We can pour out our hearts to God in prayer, and
He will listen to us with compassion and understanding. We can
be honest with Him about our fears, doubts, failures, and
insecurities, knowing that He loves us and cares for us. When we
bring our concerns to God, we can experience His peace, which
surpasses all understanding. We don't have to carry our burdens
alone or pretend that everything is okay when it's not. We can trust
that God is with us, and He will help us through whatever
challenges we face.

If you're struggling to find someone to confide in,
remember that you can always turn to God. He is always available,

and He will never turn you away. You can trust Him with your deepest concerns and fears, knowing that He is faithful and true.

NOTES:

_____

_____

_____

_____

_____

_____

_____

_____

_____

_____

_____

_____

_____

_____

_____

_____

_____

_____

_____

_____

_____

_____

FIRST COMPUTER

The first computer dates back to Adam and Eve. It was
an apple with limited memory.
Just one byte and everything crashed!

Sickness, death, hate, and murder, all are a result of the Adam
and Eve crash. More than one person has asked "If God is good,
why does He allow evil in this world? The answer is the crash. In
Romans 5:12 Paul writes "Therefore, just as through one man sin
entered into the world, and death through sin, and so death spread
to all men, because all sinned-" Our present society has told God
"Leave us alone. We will call if we need you." But when
catastrophes hit, we scream at God, "Where are you?" His reply?
"I'm right here, out of your way just like you wanted."

What can we as Christians do when faced with a Postmodern
society that rejects God yet demands to know where He is in the
midst of calamity? 2 Chronicles 7:14 provides the answer "and
My people who are called by My name humble themselves and
pray and seek My face and turn from their wicked ways, then I
will hear from heaven, will forgive their sin and will heal their
land." In Hebrew the word humble is placed at the beginning of
the sentence to call attention to the importance of Christians
humbling themselves before God. When we become humble,
pray, and seek God's way He promises to come alongside us,
forgive our sins, and offer healing throughout our land. Why not
join me today by kneeling before God in humbleness and praying
for our land to be healed.

NOTES:

_____

_____

COFFEE AND CREAMER

What did the coffee say to the creamer?
I love you a latte.

That is a funny pun that brings a smile to our faces, but it also highlights the importance of expressing love to those around us. As Christians, we are called to love one another, even when it's difficult. However, we may encounter situations where we struggle to extend that love, especially to those who have hurt us.

Perhaps you've had a friend who turned out to be an imposter seeking to discredit you. Or a business partner who betrayed your trust. Or even people in your church community who didn't live up to your expectations. It's natural to feel hurt, angry, and even resentful in such situations. But as followers of Christ, we are called to a higher standard.

Ephesians 4:32 tells us to be kind, tenderhearted, and forgiving towards one another, just as God in Christ forgave us. This can be a challenging command to follow, especially when we've been deeply wounded. But we must remember that forgiveness is not about excusing the wrong that was done to us. Rather, it's about releasing the anger, bitterness, and resentment that can consume us and prevent us from moving forward.

So how do we forgive when every ounce of our being rebels against that idea? Colossians 3:1-2 gives us the answer: "Therefore if you have been raised up with Christ, keep seeking the things above, where Christ is, seated at the right hand of God. Set your mind on the things above, not on the things that are on earth." To forgive others, we need to shift our focus from our own pain and hurt to the greater purpose that God has for our lives. We need to remember that we are called to reflect the love of Christ in all that we do, even when it's difficult. We can draw strength and guidance from God's Word and the Holy Spirit, who will empower us to extend forgiveness and love towards those who have hurt us.

The pun "I love you a latte" reminds us of the importance of expressing love to those around us. As Christians, we are called to love and forgive one another, even when it's difficult. We can draw strength and guidance from God's Word and the Holy Spirit, who will help us to focus on the greater purpose that God has for our lives. Let us choose to set our hearts and minds on things above, and extend love and forgiveness towards those who have hurt us.

NOTES:

_____

_____

_____

_____

_____

_____

_____

_____

_____

_____

_____

_____

_____

_____

_____

ALPHABET

I'm super friendly with twenty-five letters of the alphabet.
I just don't know why.

That pun is a silly play on words, but it reminds me of how we can feel about ourselves sometimes. We might think we're friendly and likable, but deep down, we wonder if we're really worth loving.

It's a common struggle for many of us, especially when we consider our own sinfulness and brokenness. We know we've messed up, made mistakes, and hurt others. We feel the weight of our failures and the darkness within us. How could anyone love us, let alone Jesus? But here's the good news: Jesus loves us precisely because we're imperfect and broken. He doesn't love us because we're "super friendly" or have it all together. In fact, in Mark 2:17 Jesus said, "...It is not those who are healthy who need a physician, but those who are sick; I did not come to call the righteous, but sinners."

Jesus came for people like you and me. He came to heal our brokenness and forgive our sins. He came to show us that love isn't based on our performance or worthiness, but on his own perfect and unconditional love for us. In Romans 5:8 the apostle Paul wrote, "But God demonstrates His own love toward us, in that while we were yet sinners, Christ died for us." Think about that for a moment. Jesus didn't wait for us to clean ourselves up or get our act together before He loved us. He loved us while we were still sinners. That's grace.

So why would Jesus love you? Because He created you, knows you, and loves you with a love that surpasses all understanding. He sees your flaws and failures, but He also sees your potential

41

and your worth. He sees you as a beloved child of God, someone who He desires to be in relationship with.

As you go about your day today, remember that Jesus loves you just as you are. You don't have to earn his love or try to be someone you're not. You can rest in the assurance that his love for you is real, powerful, and unchanging. And that, my friend, is something worth celebrating.

NOTES:

_____

_____

_____

_____

_____

_____

_____

_____

_____

_____

_____

_____

_____

_____

_____

_____

BURIAL PLOT

I saw an advertisement for burial plots and thought,
"This is the last thing I need."

When I read that pun I couldn't help but chuckle to myself and think, "This is the last thing I need!"

But as I pondered that thought, I began to realize that there is a deeper truth to it. As a Christian, what is the last thing I need? Is it material possessions, success, or fame? No, the last thing I need is to live a life without seeking God and His ways.

In Matthew 6:33, Jesus tells us, "But seek first His kingdom and His righteousness, and all these things will be added to you." What are these things that will be added? They are the things we need—food, clothing, and shelter. But Jesus says that these things will be given to us if we seek God and His righteousness first.

So often we get caught up in the pursuit of things that we think we need—a bigger house, a nicer car, a better job. But Jesus reminds us that the things we truly need come from seeking Him and His ways. When we put God first, everything else falls into place. It's easy to get distracted by the things of this world and forget what truly matters. But as we seek God first, He provides for us in ways that we could never imagine. We may not have everything we want, but we have everything we need.

The next time something you believe you need catches your eye, recall that the last thing anyone truly needs is to live a life devoid of seeking God and His ways. Prioritize Him in your life, allow Him to provide what is necessary, not just what is desired.

NOTES:

KING ARTHUR

Who invented King Arthur's round table?
Sir Conference.

Have you ever wondered who invented King Arthur's famous round table? According to this pun, it was Sir Conference. But let's think about the word "conference" for a moment. It comes from the Latin "conferre," which means "to bring together." And that's exactly what King Arthur's round table did - it brought together his knights in a spirit of unity and equality.

But as we consider King Arthur's round table we might also think of a similar word - circumference - the measurement of the distance around a circle. This measurement is an important concept in geometry and mathematics. So, which is the correct thought - Sir Conference or circumference? Perhaps they're both correct in their own way. Sir Conference brought together King Arthur's knights in a spirit of unity, while the circumference represents the unbroken and continuous nature of a circle.

As Christians, we're called to live in unity with one another, just as King Arthur's knights did. But living in unity with others can be difficult, especially when we have different opinions or ways of doing things. It's much easier to stick to our own way of thinking and doing things. But as Christians, we're called to follow God's way, even when it's difficult. In Matthew 7:13-14, Jesus says, "Enter through the narrow gate; for the gate is wide and the way is broad that leads to destruction, and there are many who enter through it. For the gate is small and the way is narrow that leads to life, and there are few who find it."

Following God's way might not be easy, but it leads to life. As G.K. Chesterton said, "The problem with Christianity is not that it has been tried and found wanting, but that it has been found difficult and left untried." Let's not be afraid to follow God's way, even when it's hard.

NOTES:

_____

_____

_____

_____

_____

_____

_____

_____

_____

_____

_____

_____

_____

_____

_____

_____

_____

_____

_____

_____

_____

_____

BEETHOVEN BACKWARD

I went to Austria to visit Beethoven's grave and heard a noise. Then I realized it was the ninth symphony being played backward. So, I asked the caretaker what was going on and he said,
"That's Beethoven, he's decomposing."

This pun is a humorous way of saying something serious: even the greatest composers eventually decompose. Just like Beethoven, death is something we can't avoid. No matter who we are, we all face the reality that one day we will leave this world behind. But what happens after that? Will we be remembered for our accomplishments, our wealth, our fame? Or will our legacy be something deeper, something that lasts beyond the grave?

As Christians, we believe that our true home is in heaven with God. When we cross the finish line of life, we will stand before Him and be rewarded with crowns for how we lived. Did we love God and love our neighbor as ourselves? Did we use our talents and resources to build His kingdom, or did we squander them on selfish pursuits?

However, it's crucial to remember that our entrance into heaven is not determined by our deeds. While our actions reflect our faith and relationship with God, it is ultimately by God's mercy and grace that we are saved. Ephesians 2:8-9 tells us it is "...by grace you have been saved through faith; and that not of yourselves, it is the gift of God; not as a result of works, so that no one may boast." Our legacy is not just about what we do, but about our faith in Christ and the work of His Spirit within us.

So, what does this have to do with Beethoven decomposing? It reminds us that our time on this earth is limited. We only have a certain number of years to live, a limited number of opportunities to make a difference. Will we waste our time on things that ultimately don't matter, or will we invest our lives in things that have eternal value? In 2 Timothy 4:7-8, the apostle Paul writes, "I have fought the good fight, I have finished the course, I have kept the faith; in the future there is laid up for me the crown of righteousness, which the Lord, the righteous Judge, will award to me on that day; and not only to me, but also to all who have loved His appearing."

Like Paul, we should strive to finish the race of life well. We should use our talents and resources to glorify God and serve others, knowing that one day we will stand before Him and hear those words: "Well done, good and faithful servant."

NOTES:

_____

_____

_____

_____

_____

_____

_____

_____

_____

_____

_____

_____

_____

_____

_____

SKELETONS AND MUSIC
B.L. Glenn

Why can't skeletons play music in church?
They have no organs.

A grocery store near my house keeps a piano on the porch. During October they set a skeleton at the piano bench and spread his hands over the keys. I've never heard music come from that piano, and certainly not from those bony hands.

When I see that skeleton sitting at the piano, the words of Isaiah come to mind, "For Sheol cannot thank You, Death cannot praise You; Those who go down to the pit cannot hope for Your faithfulness. It is the living who give thanks to You, as I do today; A father tells his sons about Your faithfulness." (Isaiah 38:18-19) The difference between us and the skeleton at the piano is that we have flesh and blood and a spirit that animates our bodies. We have the ability to sing and make music. We have a unique ability to worship God in song.

Power is found in worshiping the LORD. It gives us an advantage over our enemy, the devil. There are times in the Old Testament when God sent Israel into battle with singing. He had them start their advance with worship instead of raised weapons. In these battles, they always won. And this principle is no different in the New Testament. Paul and Silas were beaten and imprisoned in iron chains during their work in Philippi. They spent the dark hours of the night praising the LORD in song. All the prisoners were listening to them when there was a great earthquake, the foundations of the prison were shaken and all the doors were immediately opened. Then everyone's bonds fell off! Paul often told the churches to rejoice because it was a safeguard for their souls! At the end of Revelation, all of the saints of the LORD are gathered together. They are singing worship to the LORD, which sounds like the rushing of many waters! They are the ones who have overcome the schemes of the spiritual enemies of God.

In his letter to the Philippians, Paul tells us to "Rejoice in the LORD always! I will say it again, rejoice!" (Philippians 4:4) Does your soul feel unresponsive to the wonders of the LORD? Open His word, read His promises and worship Him! You are not a skeleton at a piano, you are an animated person made in the image of God. Turn your music up with your hands of flesh and praise Him today!

NOTES:

KIDNAPPING

There was a kidnapping at school the other day.
Don't worry though, he woke up.

This pun may bring a chuckle, but it also reminds us of the importance of staying awake and alert. In the same way, as believers, we must be vigilant to not fall asleep spiritually.

In 1 Thessalonians 5:6, the apostle Paul urges us to be alert and sober. He is not talking about physical wakefulness, but rather spiritual alertness. It's easy to get caught up in the distractions of daily life, like watching sports or playing games, and let our spiritual lives slip away. But just like the kid-napping who woke up, we too can wake up spiritually. We can be intentional about setting aside time to connect with God, even amidst our busy schedules. It's not about neglecting our other responsibilities or hobbies, but rather prioritizing our relationship with God. We must be diligent in guarding our hearts and minds against the things that can distract us from God. We need to be watchful of the things we allow into our lives, such as negative influences or unhealthy habits. We can't afford to let these things take over our lives and lead us astray.

So, how can we stay spiritually awake and alert? First and foremost, we need to spend time in prayer and Bible study. This means setting aside time every day to seek God's presence and guidance. It also means being open and receptive to the Holy Spirit's leading, even when it may be uncomfortable or challenging. We also need to surround ourselves with like-minded believers who can encourage and challenge us in our faith. This includes being part of a local church or small group where we can grow together and hold each other accountable. Finally, we need to be intentional about living out our faith in our daily lives. This means loving others, serving those in need, and sharing the good news of Jesus with those around us. When we live out our faith in tangible ways, we become a witness to others and bring glory to God.

As we go about our daily lives, we need to remember the pun: "There was a kidnapping at school the other day. Don't worry though, he woke up." Let's not fall asleep spiritually, but instead be alert and sober, ready to serve and follow God wherever He leads us.

NOTES:

_____

_____

_____

_____

_____

_____

_____

_____

_____

_____

_____

_____

_____

_____

_____

_____

_____

LAUGHING OCTOPUS

How many tickles does it take to make an octopus
laugh?
Tentacles.

I love to make our youngest daughter laugh. Our nightly
routine as I tuck her into bed involves me tickling her while our
fluffy white dog joins in the fun. That is the fun side of me, but I
have another side that isn't so fun. It's a side that no one had to
teach me; I was born with it. I haven't needed formal instruction
in the arts of lying, cheating, stealing, and so forth. I already knew
how to do those things. I was born ready. What I had to be taught
was how to do good, how to reach out to others when I don't want
to, and a host of other unselfish traits.

I don't think I am the only one who has faced this issue, the
question is how do we resolve this tension point in our lives?
Proverbs 22:17 provides us with a three-step solution. It says
"Incline your ear, and hear the words of the wise, and apply your
heart to my knowledge." (ESV) Here I see I must first incline or
lean toward God with the intent of hearing. Second, I must hear
instruction from wise people like Solomon, or the godly people
God has placed in my life. The third step is difficult. I need to take
what I hear and apply it to my heart (my inner essence or entire
being). This means instead of feeding the part of my nature that
lies, cheats, and steals, I feed my other nature, my godly nature. I
know I have two natures residing in me and waging war against
each other. Which one wins depends on which one I feed.

NOTES:
_____

_____

_____

NO COFFIN

Did you hear that the guy who invented the throat lozenge died?

It was announced there would be no coffin at his funeral.

Funerals are difficult for me. Sometimes they are difficult because I know the person who died was an unbeliever. Sometimes they are difficult because the person has left a hole in my heart by his or her passing. Two funerals stand out in my mind. When my father died, I held back my tears and thought I was being a son to my mother, showing her that I was strong and she could lean on me. I buried my grief inside of myself. That didn't work. The grief came out in quick bursts of anger, frustration, and condemnation of others. I was inwardly mad and frustrated that I could not show my grief. Mind you, no one told me to hold my grief inside, it's what I decided to do and the results were terrible. The second funeral was for my mother. When my aunt called to tell me I needed to make the six-hour trip to my mom's house because the doctors did not think she would last through the night, I knew deep inside myself this was mom's final struggle. As I drove those six hours, I cried as I talked with the LORD about my mother, her life, and how I would miss her. When her time came to transition to heaven, circumstances left me as the sole person at her bedside. The peace that invaded that hospital room was beyond anything I have ever experienced. My son arrived shortly after my mother left this earth and experienced a room holding a lifeless body yet filled with incredible peace. He saw my red eyes, hugged me, and said "It's okay Dad."

I firmly believe the peace I experienced came because I allowed myself to grieve and put my grief out to God. In return, God imparted the peace John writes about in the fourteenth chapter of his gospel. Here Jesus is addressing the disciples about His death. He tells them "Peace I leave with you; My peace I give to you; not as the world gives do I give to you. Do not let your heart be troubled, nor let it be fearful."

I was troubled and angry when my father died. I took my cue from the world and acted as I felt it dictated. There is no peace in what the world gives. When my mother died, I leaned on God, who left me with a peace the world is incapable of providing. There is a choice to be made when we need peace in our lives. Do we turn to the world or God? I've done both and found God's peace far more fulfilling than the world. If you need peace lean on God, He will provide what you need in abundance.

NOTES:

_____

_____

_____

_____

_____

_____

_____

_____

_____

_____

_____

_____

_____

CROSSWORDS

Don't interrupt someone working intently on a puzzle.
Chances are you will hear some crosswords.

I was once asked by a friend to attend an AA meeting to give him moral support. As I was sitting in the meeting, I heard many of the men and women speak about their struggles in dealing with life while being sober. One of their biggest challenges was saying things to others they ended up regretting. One man had created the acronym H.A.L.T. He never wanted to get too Hungry, Angry, Lonely, or Tired. If he did, he knew his choice of words had the possibility of harming others. Harming others made him feel unacceptable. Feeling unacceptable, lead him back to the drink of his choice.

What he said stuck with me. Looking at my life, I see times I am hungry, frustrated, or tired. At these times I tend to spew cross words from my mouth. As I speak, I instantly regret what I have said. To help me, I have adapted an acronym. My acronym makes no sense to others (it's HFT, Hungry, Frustrated, Tired) but it works for me.

In Colossians. 3:12-17 Paul writes "So, as those who have been chosen of God, holy and beloved, put on a heart of compassion, kindness, humility, gentleness and patience; bearing with one another, and forgiving each other, whoever has a complaint against anyone; just as the Lord forgave you, so also should you. Beyond all these things put on love, which is the perfect bond of unity. Let the peace of Christ rule in your hearts, to which indeed you were called in one body; and be thankful. Let the word of Christ richly dwell within you, with all wisdom teaching and admonishing one another with psalms and hymns and spiritual songs, singing with thankfulness in your hearts to God. Whatever you do in word or deed, do all in the name of the Lord Jesus, giving thanks through Him to God the Father."

In this passage Paul urges the Colossians, to clothe themselves with compassion, kindness, humility, gentleness, and patience. He emphasizes the importance of forgiving one another and letting love unite them. Paul encourages them to let the peace of Christ rule in their hearts and to be thankful in all circumstances. He reminds them to let the word of Christ dwell richly within them, teaching and encouraging each other with songs of praise. Ultimately, he exhorts them to do everything in the name of the Lord Jesus, with a heart overflowing with gratitude. Let's embrace these virtues, forgive freely, and spread love abundantly, knowing that through Christ, we can truly make a difference in the lives of others.

NOTES:

_____

_____

_____

_____

_____

_____

_____

_____

_____

_____

_____

_____

ARK

Need an Ark?
I Noah a guy.

Have you ever felt like the world is crashing down on you? Like a flood of problems is about to wash you away? I have. Life can be tough, but fortunately, we don't have to face it alone. We have a guy, and His name is YAHWEH.

In the book of Genesis, we read about a man named Noah. He lived in a world that was full of wickedness, and God decided to cleanse the earth with a flood. But God also showed mercy to Noah and his family by providing them with an Ark, a vessel that would keep them safe from the floodwaters.

Noah didn't have to rely on his own strength to survive the flood. He trusted in God and followed His instructions to build the Ark. And because of his faith and obedience, Noah and his family were saved from the destruction that came upon the earth. Likewise, when the storms of life come our way, we don't have to face them alone. We have a God who loves us and who is always with us. He is our refuge and our strength, a very present help in trouble (Psalm 46:1).

When we face challenges, it's easy to feel overwhelmed and hopeless. But we can take comfort in knowing that we have a God who is greater than any problem we may face. He has the power to calm the storm, to provide a way out, and to give us the strength we need to endure. If you're feeling like you need an Ark, remember that you have a guy. His name is YAHWEH, and He is with you always. Trust in Him, follow His lead, and you will find safety and peace in the midst of life's storms.

Prayer:
Heavenly Father, thank you for being with me always. Help me to trust in you and follow your lead, even when life gets tough.

Give me the strength and courage I need to face any challenge that comes my way, knowing that you are with me and that you will never leave me or forsake me. In Jesus' name, Amen.

NOTES:

_____

_____

_____

_____

_____

_____

_____

_____

_____

_____

_____

_____

_____

_____

_____

_____

_____

_____

_____

_____

IT STILL HERTZ

I injured myself measuring radio frequencies yesterday.
It still Hertz.

As Christians, we are not immune to pain and hurt. In fact, we may find ourselves injured, wounded, or hurt by God. It could be that we did not get what we asked for, or something did not turn out the way we expected. But what do we do when we find ourselves in this place? It's easy to feel as though God has failed us, isn't listening, or is absent. But as believers, we must remember that God is not the cause of our pain, but rather, He is the one who can heal it. The pun "It still Hertz" reminds us that pain and hurt may still linger, but we can trust in God's healing power.

When we come to God with our pain and hurt, we must acknowledge that we do not have all the answers, that we do not fully understand God's ways, and that we need His help. In 1 Peter 5:6-7, we are encouraged to "...humble yourselves under the mighty hand of God, that He may exalt you at the proper time, casting all your anxiety on Him, because He cares for you.." This passage tells us that when we come to God with humility, He will not reject us. Instead, He will draw us close and walk with us through our pain and struggles. He may not give us all the answers we want, but He will give us what we need: His love, His comfort, and His strength.

It's important to note that coming to God with humility does not mean that we cannot express our emotions or ask questions. God wants us to be honest with Him and to bring our whole selves to Him. He can handle our doubts, our fears, and our anger. We can cry out to Him like the psalmists did and pour out our hearts before Him.

In our pain and hurt, we can come to God with humility, trusting in His healing power and resting in the truth of His love and care for us. "It still Hertz," but we can find comfort in knowing that we are not alone and that God is with us.

NOTES:

_____

_____

_____

_____

_____

_____

_____

_____

_____

_____

_____

_____

_____

_____

_____

_____

_____

_____

_____

SUGGESTED PRAYER METHOD

I read the title of this page and I think to myself, "Great, here's another way to pray. What is the author going to do? Is he going to tell me that I have to be on my knees to show my humbleness to God so that He will hear my prayer? Is the author going to tell me that I need to incorporate scripture into every prayer to make my prayer more meaningful to God. Or is he going to tell me that I need to find a special place to pray so that I can focus in on who God is as I pray?"

When I think about praying and how I should pray I go directly to the source. By source I mean our Lord and Savior Jesus Christ. In Matthew five we find Christ going up on a mountain sitting down and teaching his disciples, not just the twelve, but as the Greek language informs us, those who were close followers. In chapter six verse nine Jesus instructs his followers on how they should pray:

"Our Father who is in heaven,
Hallowed be Your name.
'Your kingdom come.
Your will be done,
On earth as it is in heaven.
'Give us this day our daily bread.
'And forgive us our debts,
as we also have forgiven our debtors.
'And do not lead us into temptation,
but deliver us from evil.
For Yours is the kingdom
and the power and the glory forever.
Amen."

We need to take a closer look at this. The first thing I see is that there is no requirement for kneeling mentioned. I often kneel when I pray as a gesture of humility before the LORD, although kneeling is not required by scripture. Christ does not include scripture in this prayer, and He is not alone or isolated from others.

If prayer doesn't include those things, then what is required? Let's take a quick look at Jesus' prayer. The first aspect of prayer that I see shown is Adoration, "Our Father who is in heaven, Hallowed be Your name." The second thing I see in this prayer is Confession, "And forgive us our debts." Next, I see Thanksgiving "Give us this day our daily bread." Although this statement can also be seen as supplication, as I read it, it speaks to me of God providing our daily needs. I want to thank Him for doing so. Finally, I see Supplication, "Lead us not into temptation, but deliver us from evil." Supplication is defined as an act of humble prayer, entreaty, or petition. Praying continuously for God's help to overcome temptation is supplication. Notice that I capitalized and placed in bold font four words. Adoration, Confession, Thanksgiving, Supplication. The first letters of each word form an acronym. **A.C.T.S**. I wish I could take credit for that acronym but it belongs to Dr. Carl Godwin Pastor Emeritus of Calvary Community Church, Lincoln, Nebraska.

If you are wondering where to begin as you pray, why not try ACTS? Tell God how great He is…Adoration, confess any sin that is in your life known or unknown…Confession, thank Him for all that He has done and is doing for you…Thanksgiving, and then pray through your prayer list for the day…Supplication. I have found A.C.T.S. to be very helpful in structuring my prayer life and I think it will also help you.

Thank you,
Dr. Chuck
><>

PRAYER JOURNAL

Date Listed	Prayer Request	Date Answered

PRAYER JOURNAL

Date Listed	Prayer Request	Date Answered

PRAYER JOURNAL

Date Listed	Prayer Request	Date Answered

PRAYER JOURNAL

Date Listed	Prayer Request	Date Answered

PRAYER JOURNAL

Date Listed	Prayer Request	Date Answered

PRAYER JOURNAL

Date Listed	Prayer Request	Date Answered

PRAYER JOURNAL

Date Listed	Prayer Request	Date Answered

PRAYER JOURNAL

Date Listed	Prayer Request	Date Answered

PRAYER JOURNAL

Date Listed	Prayer Request	Date Answered

PRAYER JOURNAL

Date Listed	Prayer Request	Date Answered

PRAYER JOURNAL

Date Listed	Prayer Request	Date Answered

PRAYER JOURNAL

Date Listed	Prayer Request	Date Answered

PRAYER JOURNAL

Date Listed	Prayer Request	Date Answered

HOW TO MEMORIZE SCRIPTURE

Scripture memorization is an important tool for our spiritual growth, yet many of us shy away from it because we find it difficult. Just as a strong and healthy body requires exercise, a vibrant and mature faith also needs the discipline of scripture memorization. It's not that scripture memorization has been tried and found wanting; it has been found difficult and left untried.

With that in mind, how can we face scripture memorization without that sinking feeling in our stomachs? You know the feeling…I stink at this and every time I have tried, I have failed. I don't want to try again and fail again. I have good news for you! I am going to share one life changing rule (at least I found it to be life changing), and two memorization methods that I have found alleviates that sinking feeling.

Here is the rule: <u>DO NOT WORRY ABOUT HOW LONG IT TAKES TO MEMORIZE THE SCRIPTURE GOD PLACES ON YOUR HEART!</u> I placed that sentence in capital letters to stress the importance of it. I have been involved in many Bible Studies that have required scripture memorization. The study typically forced me to learn three to four verses a week. As hard as I tried, I was seldom able to meet that requirement. That lead me to feel like a failure. The bible study that was designed to help me in my spiritual growth did the opposite! I felt failure, not because I could not put into practice the concepts that were taught, but because I could not memorize the scriptures required by the study. As I have progressed in my spiritual growth, I have realized that as long as I am diligent in my effort, time does not need to be a consideration.

Here are the two memorization methods: Both stress that it is more important to memorize scripture (no matter how long it takes) rather than the number of scriptures we manage to memorize within a given time frame.

1. Choose a translation you are comfortable with. Read the passage that the verse you are memorizing is contained within. For example, if you are memorizing 1 John 1:9 "If we confess our sins, He is faithful and righteous, so that He will forgive us our sins and cleanse us from all unrighteousness," read all ten verses in 1 John chapter one. Next, read the verse you want to memorize out loud as many times as you need to get a clear understanding of what it means. When you read the verse be sure to quote the scripture reference before and after the verse. If I am memorizing 1 John 1:9 I would say out loud, "1 John 1:9, If we confess our sins, He is faithful and righteous, to forgive us our sins and to cleanse us from all unrighteousness, 1 John 1:9." Next try to memorize just the scripture reference. Once you have that down, begin memorizing the first phrase of the verse. Take your time, there is no rush. Then move on to the next phrase of the verse. Always quote the scripture reference before and after the phrase(s) you are quoting or memorizing. Next find someone (a friend, a member of your small group, etc.) who will check that you are quoting the verse correctly (be sure to let them know what translation you are using. The above quote is from the New American Standard Bible1995 Update translation). Once you can quote the verse correctly, be sure and continue to recite it so that it does not depart from your mind. At one point in my life, I was challenged to memorize Romans chapters 6,7, and 8. I find after three decades of reciting these chapters, I still need to go back and relearn some of the verses.

2. Another method that has proven successful is the "Fill In The Blank" method. Choose a translation you are

comfortable with. Let's continue to use 1 John 1:9. The first step is to write the verse out using the scripture reference before and after the verse. Next attempt to write the reference. Once you can write the reference from memory, work on the first phase of the verse. Read the verse multiple times until you understand what it is saying, then write the first word of the phrase and look at the rest of the verse. Continue using blanks for each consecutive word until you can write out the full phrase. For example, if I am memorizing 1 John 1:9 and I have begun working on the first phase of the verse, my paper would look like this: __ _____ __:___ "___ ____ _____ our sins, He is faithful and righteous, so that He will forgive us our sins and cleanse us from all unrighteousness," _ _____ __:___. When we fill in the blanks it looks like this: 1 John 1:9 "If we confess our sins, He is faithful and righteous, so that He will forgive us our sins and cleanse us from all unrighteousness, 1 John 1:9." This process is much slower than the first process, but it is effective. Remember it is not important how quickly you can memorize scripture. It is important that you find a method that works for you.

On the pages that follow, I have listed verses that I have found profitable for spiritual growth. These verses are from the New American Standard 1995 updated translation of the Bible, so you might find them hard to memorize. Please do not feel that you must use the translation I have provided.

It is vitally important that you find a translation you are comfortable with and use it to memorize from. However, let me caution you to use one translation for memorization. Early in the process of memorizing Romans 6,7, and 8, I mixed the ESV, NASB, and the KJV. The result was a very convoluted set of chapters! Here are the fifty scriptures that I have found beneficial to spiritual growth.

Thank you,
Dr. Chuck
 ><>

John 3:16 - "For God so loved the world, that He gave His only begotten Son, that whoever believes in Him shall not perish, but have eternal life."

Romans 8:28 - "And we know that God causes all things to work together for good to those who love God, to those who are called according to His purpose."

Philippians 4:13 - "I can do all things through Him who strengthens me."

Jeremiah 29:11 - "For I know the plans that I have for you,' declares the Lord, 'plans for welfare and not for calamity to give you a future and a hope."

Proverbs 3:5-6 - "Trust in the Lord with all your heart And do not lean on your own understanding. In all your ways acknowledge Him, And He will make your paths straight."

Psalm 119:11 - "Your word I have treasured in my heart, That I may not sin against You."

2 Corinthians 5:21 - "He made Him who knew no sin to be sin on our behalf, so that we might become the righteousness of God in Him."

Isaiah 40:31 - "Yet those who wait for the Lord Will gain new strength; They will mount up with wings like eagles, They will run and not get tired, They will walk and not become weary."

Matthew 6:34 - "So do not worry about tomorrow; for tomorrow will care for itself. Each day has enough trouble of its own."

Psalm 139:14 - "I will give thanks to You, for I am fearfully and wonderfully made; Wonderful are Your works, And my soul knows it very well."

John 14:6 - "Jesus said to him, 'I am the way, and the truth, and the life; no one comes to the Father but through Me.'"

Proverbs 30:5 - "Every word of God is tested; He is a shield to those who take refuge in Him."

Romans 5:8 - "But God demonstrates His own love toward us, in that while we were yet sinners, Christ died for us."

Psalm 27:1 - "The Lord is my light and my salvation; Whom shall I fear? The Lord is the defense of my life; Whom shall I dread?"

Ephesians 2:8-9 - "For by grace you have been saved through faith; and that not of yourselves, it is the gift of God; not as a result of works, so that no one may boast."

Psalm 46:1 - "God is our refuge and strength, A very present help in trouble."

Romans 12:1 – 2 - "Therefore I urge you, brethren, by the mercies of God, to present your bodies a living and holy sacrifice, acceptable to God, which is your spiritual service of worship. And do not be conformed to this world, but be transformed by the renewing of your mind, so that you may prove what the will of God is, that which is good and acceptable and perfect."

Isaiah 41:10 - "Do not fear, for I am with you; Do not anxiously look about you, for I am your God. I will strengthen you, surely I will help you, Surely I will uphold you with My righteous right hand."

1 Corinthians 10:13 - "No temptation has overtaken you but such as is common to man; and God is faithful, who will not allow you to be tempted beyond what you are able, but with the temptation will provide the way of escape also, so that you will be able to endure it."

Colossians 3:23-24 - "Whatever you do, do your work heartily, as for the Lord rather than for men, knowing that from the Lord you will receive the reward of the inheritance. It is the Lord Christ whom you serve."

Matthew 5:16 - "Let your light shine before men in such a way that they may see your good works, and glorify your Father who is in heaven."

Psalm 118:24 - "This is the day which the Lord has made; Let us rejoice and be glad in it."

James 1:2-4 - "Consider it all joy, my brethren, when you encounter various trials, knowing that the testing of your faith produces endurance. And let endurance have its perfect result, so that you may be perfect and complete, lacking in nothing."

Romans 10:9 - "That if you confess with your mouth Jesus as Lord, and believe in your heart that God raised Him from the dead, you will be saved."

Galatians 2:20 - "I have been crucified with Christ; and it is no longer I who live, but Christ lives in me; and the life which I now live in the flesh I live by faith in the Son of God, who loved me and gave Himself up for me."

Hebrews 13:8 - "Jesus Christ is the same yesterday and today and forever."

Psalm 23:1 - "The Lord is my shepherd, I shall not want."

2 Timothy 1:7 - "For God has not given us a spirit of timidity, but of power and love and discipline."

John 10:10 - "The thief comes only to steal and kill and destroy; I came that they may have life, and have it abundantly."

Philippians 2:3-4 - "Do nothing from selfishness or empty conceit, but with humility of mind regard one another as more important than yourselves; do not merely look out for your own personal interests, but also for the interests of others."

Proverbs 16:3 - "Commit your works to the Lord And your plans will be established."

1 Peter 5:7 - "casting all your anxiety on Him, because He cares for you."

Psalm 37:4 - "Delight yourself in the Lord; And He will give you the desires of your heart."

Matthew 22:37-39 - "And He said to him, 'You shall love the Lord your God with all your heart, and with all your soul, and with all your mind.' This is the great and foremost commandment. The second is like it, 'You shall love your neighbor as yourself.'"

Isaiah 53:5 - "But He was pierced through for our transgressions, He was crushed for our iniquities; The chastening for our well-being fell upon Him, And by His scourging we are healed."

1 John 4:7 - "Beloved, let us love one another, for love is from God; and everyone who loves is born of God and knows God."

Psalm 46:10 - "Cease striving and know that I am God; I will be exalted among the nations, I will be exalted in the earth."

Colossians 3:12-13 - "So, as those who have been chosen of God, holy and beloved, put on a heart of compassion, kindness, humility, gentleness and patience; bearing with one another, and forgiving each other, whoever has a complaint against anyone; just as the Lord forgave you, so also should you.

Psalm 119:105 - "Your word is a lamp to my feet And a light to my path."

Acts 14:6 - "Jesus said to him, 'I am the way, and the truth, and the life; no one comes to the Father except through Me.'"

Proverbs 17:22 - "A joyful heart is good medicine But a broken spirit dries up the bones."

Isaiah 43:1 - "But now, thus says the LORD your Creator, O Jacob, And He who formed you, O Israer, 'do not fear, for I have redeemed you; I have called you by name; you are Mine!'"

Philippians 4:6-7 - "Be anxious for nothing, but in everything by prayer and supplication with thanksgiving let your requests be made known to God. And the peace of God, which surpasses all comprehension, will guard your hearts and your minds in Christ Jesus."

Proverbs 27:17 - "Iron sharpens iron, So one man sharpens another."

Ephesians 6:10-11 - "Finally, be strong in the Lord and in the strength of His might. Put on the full armor of God, so that you will be able to stand firm against the schemes of the devil."

Isaiah 43:2 - "When you pass through the waters, I will be with you; And through the rivers, they will not overflow you. When you walk through the fire, you will not be scorched, Nor will the flame burn you."

Matthew 6:33 - "But seek first His kingdom and His righteousness, and all these things will be added to you."

1 Corinthians 13:4-7 - "Love is patient, love is kind and is not jealous; love does not brag and is not arrogant, does not act unbecomingly; it does not seek its own, is not provoked, does not take into account a wrong suffered, does not rejoice in unrighteousness, but rejoices with the truth; bears all things, believes all things, hopes all things, endures all things."

Isaiah 43:25 - "I, even I, am the one who wipes out your transgressions for My own sake; And I will not remember your sins."

Romans 3:23 - "For all have sinned and fall short of the glory of God,"

Hebrews 4:12 - "For the word of God is living and active and sharper than any two-edged sword, and piercing as far as the division of soul and spirit, of both joints and marrow, and able to judge the thoughts and intentions of the heart."

Matthew 11:28-30 - "Come to Me, all who are weary and heavy-laden, and I will give you rest. Take My yoke upon you and learn from Me, for I am gentle and humble in heart, and you will find rest for your souls. For My yoke is easy and My burden is light."

John 8:32 - "and you will know the truth, and the truth will make you free."

2 Timothy 3:16-17 - "All Scripture is inspired by God and profitable for teaching, for reproof, for correction, for training in righteousness; so that the man of God may be adequate, equipped for every good work."

Proverbs 2:6 - "For the Lord gives wisdom; From His mouth come knowledge and understanding."

Colossians 3:1-3 - "If then you have been raised up with Christ, keep seeking the things above, where Christ is, seated at the right of God. Set your mind on the thing above, not on the things that are on earth. For you have died and your life is hidden with Christ in God."

Psalm 121:1-2 - "I will lift up my eyes to the mountains; From where shall my help come? My help comes from the Lord, Who made heaven and earth."

Proverbs 15:1 - "A gentle answer turns away wrath, But a harsh word stirs up anger."

Galatians 5:22-23 - "But the fruit of the Spirit is love, joy, peace, patience, kindness, goodness, faithfulness, gentleness, self-control; against such things there is no law."

Psalm 34:8 - "O taste and see that the Lord is good; How blessed is the man who takes refuge in Him!"

Proverbs 1:7 - " The fear of the LORD is the beginning of knowledge; Fools despise wisdom and instruction."

Titus 3:5 – "He saved us, not on the basis of deeds which we have done in righteousness, but according to His mercy, by the washing of regeneration and renewing by the Holy Spirit."

2 Timothy 3:16 – "All scripture is inspired by God and profitable for teaching, for reproof, for correction, for training in righteousness;"

Psalm 103:2-5 - "Bless the Lord, O my soul, And forget none of His benefits; Who pardons all your iniquities, Who heals all your diseases; Who redeems your life from the pit, Who crowns you with lovingkindness and compassion; Who satisfies your years with good things, So that your youth is renewed like the eagle."

Joshua 1:9 – "Have I not commanded you? Be strong and courageous! Do not tremble or be dismayed, for the LORD your God is with you wherever you go.

Matthew 28:19-20 - "Go therefore and make disciples of all the nations, baptizing them in the name of the Father and the Son and the Holy Spirit, teaching them to observe all that I commanded you; and lo, I am with you always, even to the end of the age."

Psalm 103:8 - "The Lord is compassionate and gracious, Slow to anger and abounding in lovingkindness."

Ephesians 4:2 - "with all humility and gentleness, with patience, showing tolerance for one another in love,"

Proverbs 4:23 - "Watch over your heart with all diligence, For from it flow the springs of life."

1 Corinthians 15:58 - "Therefore, my beloved brethren, be steadfast, immovable, always abounding in the work of the Lord, knowing that your toil is not in vain in the Lord."

Romans 6:1 - "What shall we say then? Are we to continue in sin so that grace may increase?"

Romans 6:2 - "May it never be! How shall we who died to sin still live in it?"

Romans 6:3 - "Or do you not know that all of us who have been baptized into Christ Jesus have been baptized into His death?"

Romans 6:4 - "Therefore we have been buried with Him through baptism into death, so that as Christ was raised from the dead through the glory of the Father, so we too might walk in newness of life."

Romans 6:5 - "For if we have become united with Him in the likeness of His death, certainly we shall also be in the likeness of His resurrection,"

Romans 6:6 - "knowing this, that our old self was crucified with Him, in order that our body of sin might be done away with, so that we would no longer be slaves to sin."

Romans 6:7 - "for he who has died is freed from sin."

Romans 6:8 - "Now if we have died with Christ, we believe that we shall also live with Him,"

Romans 6:9 - "knowing that Christ, having been raised from the dead, is never to die again; death no longer is master over Him."

Romans 6:10 - "For the death that He died, He died to sin once for all; but the life that He lives, He lives to God."

Romans 6:11 - "Even so consider yourselves to be dead to sin, but alive to God in Christ Jesus."

Romans 6:12 - "Therefore do not let sin reign in your mortal body so that you obey its lusts,"

Romans 6:13 - "and do not go on presenting the members of your body to sin as instruments of unrighteousness; but present yourselves to God as those alive from the dead, and your members as instruments of righteousness to God."

Romans 6:14 - "For sin shall not be master over you, for you are not under law but under grace."

Romans 6:15 - "What then? Shall we sin because we are not under law but under grace? May it never be!"

Romans 6:16 - "Do you not know that when you present yourselves to someone as slaves for obedience, you are slaves of the one whom you obey, either of sin resulting in death, or of obedience resulting in righteousness?"

Romans 6:17 - "But thanks be to God that though you were slaves of sin, you became obedient from the heart to that form of teaching to which you were committed,"

Romans 6:18 - "and having been freed from sin, you became slaves of righteousness."

Romans 6:19 - "I am speaking in human terms because of the weakness of your flesh. For just as you presented your members as slaves to impurity and to lawlessness, resulting in further lawlessness, so now present your members as slaves to righteousness, resulting in sanctification."

Romans 6:20 - "For when you were slaves of sin, you were free in regard to righteousness."

Romans 6:21 - "Therefore what benefit were you then deriving from the things of which you are now ashamed? For the outcome of those things is death."

Romans 6:22 - "But now having been freed from sin and enslaved to God, you derive your benefit, resulting in sanctification, and the outcome, eternal life."

Romans 6:23 - "For the wages of sin is death, but the free gift of God is eternal life in Christ Jesus our Lord."

CONTACT INFORMATION

Moments With Yahweh

1001 West Grassland Lane

Lincoln, NE 68522

Phone: 402-613-5826

Email: contacts@mwy4chuck.com

Reference: A Refreshing Chuckle II

www.ingramcontent.com/pod-product-compliance
Lightning Source LLC
Chambersburg PA
CBHW070819050426
42452CB00011B/2106